SUNDAY NEWS
NEW YORK'S PICTURE NEWSPAPER
August 6, 1939

DOROTHY LAMOUR

STRIKING POSES

RICHARD SCHICKEL

PHOTOGRAPHS FROM
THE KOBAL COLLECTION

PICTURE EDITORS

SIMON CROCKER
CAROL RUBINSTEIN

STEWART, TABORI & CHANG
NEW YORK

Text copyright © 1987 Gideon Productions Inc.

Photographs copyright © 1987 The Kobal Collection (NY) Ltd.

Published by Stewart, Tabori & Chang, Inc.
740 Broadway, New York, New York 10003

LIBRARY OF CONGRESS CATALOGING-IN-PUBLICATION DATA

Schickel, Richard.
    Striking poses.

    1. Moving-picture actors and actresses—Portraits.
2. Kobal Collection.   3. Photograph collections—
England—London.   I. Crocker, Simon.   II. Rubinstein,
Carol.   III. Kobal Collection.   IV. Title.
PN1998.A2S35   1987   791.43′028′0922 [B]   86-23187
ISBN 0-941434-97-4 (cloth)
ISBN 1-55670-024-5 (paper)

Distributed by Workman Publishing
1 West 39 Street, New York, New York 10018

Printed in Japan

 88 89 10 9 8 7 6 5 4 3 2

Design: J.C. Suarès
         Diana M. Jones

CONTENTS

Don't laugh. Don't even smile. These pictures were not meant to be funny.

The motion picture studios that spent small fortunes to make and distribute these images thirty, forty, fifty years ago did not think they were funny. In fact, they were a key element in the very earnest process by which studios built up contract players to star status—and then kept them there. They were certainly not funny to the still photographers who obviously expended large amounts of technical skill and a certain fecundity of imagination on composing them. Above all, they were not funny to the people who posed for them. They saw these pictures as a form of degradation. For it was when they were alone in the stills studio, with only the tough-talking lensman and the placatory gal from the publicity department to guide them, that they felt the wheels of the factory grinding most deeply into their often half-naked flesh.

It was here more than anywhere else on the lot that image subsumed individuality and a person was made to feel that he or she was only a paper-doll persona up in a cardboard sky, representing not his or her own uniqueness, but a corporate version of it, something being cut and shaped to fit a predetermined mold, a salable type.

This one should smoulder. That one's a sizzler. Here's a little homebody. He's definitely the outdoor type. She speaks to us of big-city streets. And so on. Leslie Caron, for example, was in her own words "the pert little *Parisienne*"—except that in her own mind she was a sober, thoughtful young woman, quite mature for her age and entirely "revolted by their emphasis on pink and lace, and their idea of femininity, which was dumbness." Much good it did her, for, as she would later tell oral historian Donald Knox, "There was always at the bottom of my pictures the caption *ooh la la*. I have a book of those nauseating pictures with *ooh la la* written down there." She also worked with poinsettias for Christmas, waded thigh-deep in a freshet to welcome the spring, and fondled many a housecat when someone decided that her beauty was of the feline variety. Finally, she "perted" out. "When I escaped that factory . . . I refused to smile for about a year, no matter how happy I would be."

Caron speaks for every performer who was subjected to routine processing by the American movie studio system in the era when it was truly a system. Whatever retrospective pleasure they may occasionally find in their on-screen work, very few of them have a kind memory for their sessions with the stillsmen, and for reasons that are far from frivolous.

In fairness, it should perhaps be noted that even if the photographers had not been functionaries of a frequently insensitive

Rita Hayworth posing to promote *The Loves of Carmen*, Columbia, 1948.

system, even if they had been artists of the most profound and delicate sensibility, the match between them and these particular subjects could never have been frictionless. To put the matter simply, actors are not at their happiest when they are required to be motionless and silent. They may become icons to us, but in their own minds they never are. What they are selling is animation in all its aspects: the play of gesture, expression, and voice, through which they convey a range of emotion no single image can hope to approximate. If we become a simpering mass of insecurities, a giggle, an inane grin, and a tangle of maladaptive limbs when we are merely asked to present an aspect of ourselves to Aunt Betsy's Polaroid, think how much more difficult it is for a performer—proud to be mercurial, proud of his ability to impersonate dozens of people in hundreds of moods—to flash-freeze a simpleton's idea of himself for the lens. Especially when that simpleton is some anonymous flack in a suit from the front office.

But having made due allowance for the inherent difficulties of temperament that performers inevitably brought to this enterprise, we must also admit that they were also inherently correct about it, morally speaking. These pictures for the most part did carelessly objectify them, did therefore dehumanize them.

We can, perhaps, see this more clearly now than we did when these images proliferated. For there was a time when they did not appear in the splendid, thought-provoking isolation that we have arranged for them here. In their day these images swam before our eyes by the hundreds every week—in the Sunday newspaper color supplements, in the barber shop's *Click*, in the beauty parlor's *Photoplay*, on billboards and calendars, anywhere an idle glance might fall. Then they were simply bright splashes in the media wallpaper of the age. Indeed, in the late '30s and early '40s the eye was still quite innocently bedazzled by color photography. Color film had been on the market only since 1935 (the same year three-stripe Technicolor was first used in a feature film), and people were so entranced by its novelty that they uncritically accepted the limitations it imposed on photographers—the harsh, unrealistic light they had to pour on a subject, the hard-edged contrasts they had to arrange in order to record an image that, in turn, could be reproduced legibly by the murky lithographic processes available to most publications. One or two sophisticates among us may even have understood that it was out of these limitations that the unique mannerisms of the classic publicity still grew. But most did not.

For the most part, our eyes unblinkingly, quite innocently accepted the conventions and stylizations of these images. They simply flickered and passed on, leaving us pleased to have seen a familiar face and form, glad to have met the comely new ones being leggily offered for our pleasure. The movies themselves may

Marilyn Monroe on the set of *How to Marry a Millionaire*,
20th Century–Fox, 1953.

have helped train our sight to this acceptance of the outrageous. Sober souls in and out of the business kept calling the medium to account in those days, urging upon it a deeper involvement with pressing issues of the moment, greater "realism" in bringing them before the audience. ("Grim death gargling at you around every streetcorner," cries the title director in Preston Sturges's *Sullivan's Travels,* urging his studio bosses to make "a commentary on modern conditions" when all they want him to do is turn out more films like his past hits *Hey, Hey in the Hayloft* and *Ants in Your Plants of 1939).* The movies, obviously, had developed their own peculiar—not to say giddy, not to say quite unrealistic—narrative conventions and visual stylizations, and, having learned to accept performers in those curious contexts, we had no difficulty accepting them in the even odder ones arranged by the publicity department. That seemed to be what people did in Hollywood—shake free the bonds of the ordinary. Well, more power to them. The ordinary is not all it's cracked up to be, not if you are mired in provincial gloom somewhere. Someone like Graham Greene, then a humble movie critic, might write that "if colour is to be of permanent importance a way must be found to use it realistically. . . . It must be made to contribute to our sense of truth." But that just shows what *he* knew. They could have splashed all the unrealistic color (or even colour) on us they wanted. Gotta feel good after all this gray.

Thus it was that the eyes passed no alarming messages to the brain, which, not yet trained to higher illiteracy by universal college education, was similarly passive. It was mildly curious about

the facts (Mona *who?* Olga San *what?*), but it had heard nothing
in those days about such concepts as "mannerisms," "convention,"
"stylization." These were not taught in any of the public schools
we attended. The documentary aesthetic, then the ruling critical
consideration in still photography, the tenets of which were clearly
being violently violated by the movie stillsmen, was not in the
forefront of consciousness either. We also might have observed that
these portraits revealed nothing of character or of social conditions, but that was scarcely to the point, was it? Nor, finally, was
the mind as quick to politicize as it has become in more recent
times. It tended to accept these photographic offerings quite lit-
erally for what they were—publicity, a necessary evil or a minor
benison, depending on your point of view (and degree of cynicism)
about show biz in a capitalist society. Anyway, nothing to get
worked up about. And since few of us were radicals—and those few
were automatically and generally contemptuous of the movies'
escapist ways and thus saw no need to analyze closely the particular workings of the "industry"—the notion that a form of human
exploitation was taking place in plain sight of every newspaper
reader in America occurred to almost no one.

ABOVE: Joan Crawford—the fans loved her—1955.
OPPOSITE: cutting the cake for *Click* Magazine, 1938.

Sorry about that. And glad, now, to apologize to the subjects of these pictures for our former insensitivity. You poor dears. How could we have been so blind? What could we have been thinking? More to the point, what could we have *not* been thinking? Oh, wondrous are the sly and silent workings of time, forcing us now to see these photographs not as the familiar furnishings of our former dailiness but as precious artifacts, loosed as if by the archeologist's trowel from the dust of that exotic land that the past always eventually becomes, demanding of us émigrés from that country that we no longer take them—and, most important, the spiritual contortions their creation imposed on their subjects—for granted.

But—what's this?—somebody over there is grinning. And you in the back row there, did I hear you snickering? Hey, you kids, cut that out. This is a serious socio-political-psychological seminar. Ms. Fonda hasn't even begun to outline the feminist position on this matter. I myself have my paper "The Ektachroming of Ecstasy" yet to present. So just settle down.

The kids won't, of course. They haven't the faintest idea of what we're talking about. We have amends to make for our careless initial reception of these pictures because we also carried on in our ever-fantasizing adolescent minds relationships of some sweet substance with their subjects. When we talk about them now—and we do—we heed the curtain-line admonition of Laura, heroine of another telling cultural artifact, *Tea and Sympathy*, and we are "kind." We wish to treat them with the tenderness memory quite properly extends to all our lost loves.

Such niceties, however, are lost on newer generations. They have no nostalgic pleasantries to extend to any of the figures represented in this book, for, with the exception of Ronald Reagan, they are but shadows flitting through the late show's dimness, rumors of wonderfulness circulated by their parents, the obscure objects of someone else's long-gone desires. We see a not unpleasant yet nonetheless dislocating image of Barbara Stanwyck and wonder how they talked that crisp, no-nonsense lady into posing for it. They see the same picture and it becomes an abstraction, "Woman with Canoe." We see mumbly earnest Glenn Ford in a smoking jacket, pulling on a pipe while his hand rests on a figure of Buddha, and we wonder if he and his employers were having us on all those years. A younger person looks at it and sees "Bourgeois Gentleman (Anonymous)." We see a wartime picture of pretty Ella Raines and drop into reverie—whatever became of her? A yuppie sees the same photograph and it becomes "Arrangement of Flags with Girl."

And so it goes. A kind of apotheosis of objectification is here attained. And a bitter irony is hinted at, for history is once again

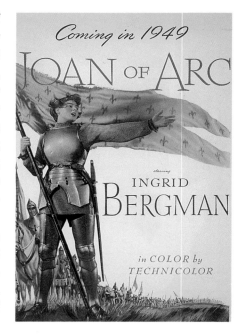

ABOVE AND OPPOSITE: the advertisement and the publicity shot for Ingrid Bergman's *Joan of Arc*, RKO, 1948.

Natalie Wood, 1960.

proved wayward in its workings. It reinforces the worst imaginings of the subjects of these photographs as they twisted and turned uncomfortably under the studio lights, or suffered the invasion of their homes by the photogs (who, often enough, brought some props along to improve on dinky reality), or leaned back farther, farther on a hot rock at Malibu, obeying instructions that had as their hidden agenda getting them to tip their tits higher, higher until they had correctly proved some imaginary hypothesis of desirability.

Their living presences no longer available to us on the screen, their imaginary presences no longer available to our idling minds, the subjects of these photographs have truly become what they most feared becoming—a palette of flesh tones, their true identities, their aspirations, their anxieties of no more consequence to us than those of the models who sat for Rembrandt or Renoir. Indeed, their historical condition is somewhat worse than that of a painter's model. For the model is at least transformed—and often transfigured—by an artist, her identity subsumed (and her anonymity guaranteed) by the approach to archetypicality.

Conversely, history now beams a kindly, welcoming smile on the growling technicians who took these pictures—so often working under the direction of publicists, former newshawks who found more comfortable nests in fine-feathered Hollywood than any city room could provide. At best barely tolerated in their time, more often patronized by many performers to their faces and scorned when their backs were turned, the photographers now find prints of their works collected by a knowledgeable cult and, of course, the subject of *Striking Poses* and many another volume. Who could have foreseen such a turnabout? For that matter, who could have imagined, a half-century ago, even a quarter-century ago, that history—austere Clio—would turn into a painted hussy, insisting that the heedlessly machined junk of former years constitutes a treasure-trove of collectibles for the nostalgia market, that many a formerly ignored or despised object actually has a mysterious resonance, an unexpected capacity to enchant not merely the memoirist but the impeccable intelligences of lofty critics?

But so it has happened. Deco pieces that could not be given away two decades ago now fetch heart-stopping prices in New York's SoHo and along L.A.'s Melrose Avenue. We must now subject to learned analysis the myth, the reality, and the gap between of pop pantheon figures like Marilyn, who have achieved truly iconographic status. Exegetes flock to the lost episodes of "The Honeymooners." And suddenly the works of the Hollywood studio photographers take on a certain glow for the observer, who has been rendered objective and objectifying by the passing years. The instant we apprehend that the historical conditions that combined

Ronald Reagan and Rhonda Fleming in *Tropic Zone*, Paramount, 1953.

OPPOSITE, CLOCKWISE FROM TOP LEFT: Audrey Hepburn filming *Sabrina*, Paramount, 1954; Natalie Wood and James Dean chat during *Rebel Without a Cause*, Warner Bros., 1955; Tony Perkins and Jane Fonda on the set of *Tall Story*, Warner Bros., 1960; Janet Leigh relaxes with daughters Jamie Lee and Kelly during *Bye Bye Birdie*, Columbia, 1963.

Anita Ekberg, *Screaming Mimi*, Columbia, 1958.

to cause any significant (or merely singular) popular-culture phenomenon cannot be reassembled, that the thing is safely dead, the
phenomenon becomes a safe investment both for our cash (if there
is a residue of physical objects that can be acquired) and for our
analytical energies (the thing cannot stir and change shape on us,
thus upsetting our theories).

In the case of Hollywood's color publicity stills, we know that
the old system—under which players were under long-term contract to the studios and could be ordered, on pain of suspension
(or, at the least, bad parts and indifference in the commissary), to
place themselves at the mercy of the photographers—is forever
buried. Stars move about in the world on their own recognizance
now, just like grown-ups, and have to be treated most respectfully
—generally through emissaries—by anyone who wants to snap
their picture when they are at work. *Their* problem with photographers is not that someone will force them to appear in the false
light of a forced pose, but that some *paparazzo* will grab an off-
guard shot of them that is all too true to life. Styles of intrusion
change, like everything else.

This particular trend took a while to arrive, and, like the stylizations of the color publicity shot, it was determined very largely
by technological developments—a rather long chain of them. At
roughly the same time that color film became a reality, so did
lightweight 35-mm cameras and black-and-white film of ever-

PRECEDING PAGES: Fred MacMurray, Jean Arthur,
Melvyn Douglas, and (seated at left) director Wesley
Ruggles filming *Too Many Husbands*, Columbia, 1940.

Cleo Moore, c. 1951.

increasing speed. One could now photograph intense action with available light, and the photo coverage of World War II—particularly in *Life*—attracted a vast audience for the immediacy and intimacy of this kind of camera work and made heroic figures, celebrities, of photojournalists. After the war, when these photographers were between grander (and gorier) assignments, they became familiars on the movie sets of the world, and the behind-the-scenes coverage of movie stars at work that these journalistic stars provided set the new standard for publicity photography. Since the studios were shutting down their stills departments (along with their other craft and service units) in response to the straitened economic conditions in which they found themselves (the result of competition from television and of the loss of their hugely profitable theater chains because of antitrust action), the fact that these new men were free-lancers, hirable by the job, also commended them both to movie makers and to magazines. By the early '60s their manner had routed the old one in the movie publicity field, reducing its former practitioners either to precarious retirement or to equally precarious employment in the less exalted reaches of the skin trade—such as calendar art—which still had use for their high-key skills. In any event, the subsequent arrival of high-speed color film placed the newer generations of photographers in a position to provide editors and readers with absolutely everything they wanted—that is to say, intimacy *and* a glitzy image. It really wasn't their fault that the market for the on-set photo story declined with the passing of the quality picture magazines. Nor was it their fault that the *paparazzi* could use the same

Paul Newman and Joanne Woodward filming against a back
projection for *From the Terrace*, 20th Century–Fox, 1960.

technology and techniques for more dubious purposes, bringing
us to our present pretty pass.

All of this, perhaps, has no direct bearing on our subject—except
for one thing: in this realm, as in all others, it is necessary for any
highly distinctive style to fall entirely out of fashion—to endure a
long season of contempt and ridicule and an equally long period in
Coventry, where it speaks to no one and no one speaks to, or of, it—
before it can be rediscovered and its strengths appreciated.

About these pictures, it is wise, I think, to be modest in our
claims. Tempting as it is to see something of the spirit of surrealism moving through some of them, and though there are one or
two shots in this book that quite obviously ape that manner, the
fact remains that, popular as the dream-factory metaphors have
always been in dealing with the movies, commerce schemes but
does not dream and therefore does not produce the raw materials
requisite for surrealistic work. If we can link these stills to any

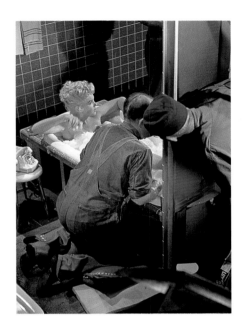

Marilyn Monroe in a tub for *The Seven Year Itch*, 20th
Century-Fox, 1955.

tradition, it is probably to that of magazine illustration. Since
before the turn of the century, commercial painters had been
producing firmly outlined, cheerily colored anecdotes, in which
prettier-than-life boys and girls were seen trimming the Christmas
tree or goin' a-fishin', or just looking perkily available for anti-
septic romance. This is not, however, a tradition likely to excite
hearts yearning to claim high respectability for these stills of ours.

It is better, perhaps, to see them as precursors. Here our possibilities are richer. Pop art, for example, clearly borrowed poses and
palette from the stillsmen, pretended to distance itself satirically
from its source, but actually got quite cozy with it. And hard-
edged photorealism, so much of which we see today in the chic
galleries nestling alongside the nostalgia shops in our trendier
urban venues, owes something to the movie magazines that kept
the artists company when they were down with the mumps and
measles in their impressionable years.

But really, what's the point of all that? This business of attrib-
uting value to works of popular art by asserting their influential
connection with the higher arts is quite tiresome. The movies, for
example, do not rise in my estimation because James Joyce once
managed a cinema and because, as a result, the structure of films
clearly had an effect on that of *Ulysses*. It may actually lower
the movies in my regard to think that their publicity materials
have shaped Andy Warhol's sensibility. The movies are their own
reward, intrinsically worthy of study as well as delight.

It follows from this belief that the corporate culture that produces them is worth attending to—especially, I think, the odd corporate culture that also produced, along with billions of moving images, these comparatively few frozen ones. For Hollywood, in the years we are discussing, commanded the attention of the world as no cultural institution and only a few religious and political movements ever have. In trying to determine how it accomplished this astonishing feat, it seems to me that these stills have become an invaluable tool. Movies, after all, are full of distracting narrative bustle. Moreover, they are evanescent. The minute we leave the theater, the film we have just seen begins to recede from our consciousness, placing more and more distance between itself and laggard memory with each passing moment. In the end, all we are left with is an impression, often a false one, and, even in the age of the video cassette, one that is difficult to refresh.

These stills, though are, well, still. They have no capacity to distract us from their true business with talk or movement or complexities of plot and characterization. They must make whatever point they have to make simply and quickly through the use of bold and simplifying and instantly readable symbols, unambiguously lit and arrestingly colored. Designed to invade our attention, they cannot afford to evade direct statement. They have no *politesse* and no pretense. They document universal desires without dither. Here is beautiful woman. Here is gorgeous man. Here is nature without a cloud in the sky. Here is sport without pain or defeat. Here is leisure without guilt. Here are holidays without family tension. Here are the lifestyles of the rich and famous with the anxiety airbrushed out. We wanted all that then, and want it still, with undiminished fervor. Now that time has passed, and those who contributed the human element to these compositions have receded from our memory—many of them receded, alas, to dust—the purity of these abstractions, the purity of our response to them, is finally perfected.

Don't laugh? Impossible. We must laugh. At the primitiveness of the calculation that went into these images, of course. But most of all at the immortal child in each of us, whose yearnings those calculations were aimed to arouse and satisfy. He lives, that whining infant, and these pictures—freeze-frames lifted from the old and half-forgotten dreams of impossible fulfillment that shrewd commerce once produced for us—put us back in touch with him. In the end, our laughter must be the laughter of self-recognition.

Barbara Stanwyck, *You Belong to Me*, Columbia, 1941.

24

This was basic, inescapable. When all was said and done on the set, when the last retakes were completed and the last loop line recorded, the movie's star always had one last acting chore to perform: to go into the stills department and try to create a single image that would attractively—if not necessarily fairly—characterize his or her latest characterization.

This was a task of no small importance, for the search here was not just for some 8×10s that the newspapers might enjoy running, but for a vision that could carry an entire advertising campaign. Sometimes, of course, this matter could be attended to without loss of dignity, as witness Cary Grant (opposite). But then, Grant was Grant, and the picture he was aiding was a rather dignified comedy, The Bishop's Wife, in which he was cast as an angel, no less. More often, the publicists were working on something as lacking in singularity (and thus in striking imagistic possibilities) as The Vanquished and had no choice but to surround John Payne's none-too-impressive bare chest with lovelies and hope for the best.

How much worse Kid Rodelo must have been we can perhaps deduce from the fact that Janet Leigh was asked to don antithetical belts (gun and garter) in hopes of recruiting an audience for it. We knew by then (1965) that, though a good sport might agree to pose in such a get-up, no one could act in it. Which meant that the still was bound to be better than the movie.

OPPOSITE: Cary Grant with harp, to promote *The Bishop's Wife*, Goldwyn, 1947.
PAGE 28: Jerry Lewis—*The Nutty Professor*—with Stella Stevens, Paramount, 1963 *(top)*; Kim Novak's *Vertigo* pose, Columbia, 1958 *(bottom left)*; Ann Sheridan for *Torrid Zone*, Warner Bros., 1940 *(bottom right)*.
PAGE 29: Humphrey Bogart, *Deadline USA*, 20th Century-Fox, 1952.
PAGE 30: Janet Leigh in character for *Kid Rodelo*, Paramount, 1965.
PAGE 31: Marlon Brando for *One-Eyed Jacks*, Paramount, 1961.
PAGE 32: Jan Sterling, John Payne, and Coleen Gray posing to promote *The Vanquished*, Paramount, 1953.
PAGE 33: Charlton Heston and Richard Rober for *The Savage*, Paramount, 1952.

ittle pets with their little pets. Imagery of this kind is almost as old as the movies. D. W. Griffith always liked to have his female discoveries (Mary Pickford, Lillian Gish, et al.) seen toying with dear, innocent creatures. Indeed, until the movies began to talk, few American women were portrayed, on screen or in stills, as possessing more mature or dangerous sexual attitudes. European women were imported to undertake that duty. Such attitudes died hard, as these pictures prove—many of them were taken in the '50s and '60s.

Obviously, it is appropriate to portray a child star with a cuddlesome domestic creature. (Elizabeth Taylor, as an adolescent, really had a pet chipmunk named Nibbles, about whom she wrote a little book.) But in recent times we have learned that there is something patronizing about showing grown women at play with birds and butterflies and puppies—or, worse, with stuffed toys. A feminist might well want to cite many of these pictures as evidence of the long history of an unconscious (or semiconscious) male need to see women as children, dependents. But we might at least marginally prefer the pictures of actresses disporting themselves on bearskins or with a large, dangerous creature in the background. If you are going to be objectified by the camera, at least let it be in the company of symbols that suggest a grown-up's sexuality.

Elizabeth Taylor and Nibbles the chipmunk, c. 1945.

OPPOSITE: Armida and her parrot, 1941.

OPPOSITE: Maureen O'Hara, c. 1942.
ABOVE: Shirley Temple, 1937.
FAR RIGHT: Margaret O'Brien, with Lassie, c. 1946.
RIGHT: Jane Withers, 1940.

Joan Collins cute—with a stuffed poodle, c. 1954.

Lana Turner astride a fake donkey to promote *Mr. Imperium*, 1951.

OPPOSITE: Esther Williams and butterfly, c. 1942.

ABOVE: Olga San Juan, c. 1944.
OPPOSITE: Elsa Martinelli plugs *Rampage*, 1963.

ABOVE: Joan Collins coy—on a bearskin rug for *The Girl in the Red Velvet Swing*, 1954.
OPPOSITE: Carroll Baker, c. 1964.

Patriotism may be the last refuge of the scoundrel, but it is the first thought of the old-fashioned publicist: how to wrap clients in the flag. The winds of war were never so ill that a zephyr could not be diverted so as to enticingly lift the skirt of *Esther Williams* (opposite), *whose photograph—caught in this giggly predicament—would, in turn, lift the morale of our horny warriors wherever the defense of freedom took them.*

Indeed, so well publicized were the salutary effects of pin-up pictures on the American soldier's will to fight that, during World War II, it would have seemed downright unpatriotic for an actress to refuse to pose for them. Or for the photographs aimed at enlisting the home front in the various drives, appeals, and activities that we were daily assured would bring the boys home sooner. In those days, the Hollywood stills departments were veritable war plants, and the women working under their lights were so many Rosies, riveting our attention to our quite pleasant duties while distracting our sons and brothers from their deadly ones. Who is to say these pin-ups did not do more to shorten the conflict than most of us did? Certainly no one can deny that they created an immortal iconography of total war—one that never was, and never will be, duplicated.

Laraine Day, 1942.

Victor Mature, 1943.

OPPOSITE: Esther Williams, *Skirts Ahoy!*, 1952.
PAGE 46: Ella Raines with the flags of the United Nations, 1945.
PAGE 47: Ann Miller, all-American girl, c. 1943.
PAGE 48: Jane Withers with badges, c. 1943.
PAGE 49: Jinx Falkenberg with medallions, c. 1944.
PAGE 50: Ann Sothern with her victory garden, c. 1943.
PAGE 51: Mary Martin, 1943.

Jean Simmons, c. 1954.

Gene Tierney had astonishing cheekbones. Sometimes they hinted to the studio bosses of enigmatic Asia, and so she was subjected to half-caste casting in items like The Shanghai Gesture. *Sometimes they merely suggested good domestic breeding, and they had her play problematical society girls of the nearer East in pictures like* Laura *and* Leave Her to Heaven. *But either way, Gene Tierney was a mystery to their Royal Crudenesses and they wanted her to be a mystery to us—hence the Daliesque portrait* (opposite), *perhaps the only conscious attempt at surrealism amidst all the unconscious ones gathered in these pages.*

One can understand why Tierney puzzled Hollywood, for she was, in fact, born to privilege, educated in finishing schools, and incorporated by her stockbroker father before she got her first movie contract. Not many women of her sophisticated social class— and reserve—went into the movies. In any event, perfect beauty has a cooling effect on audiences as well as on movie moguls, so Tierney remained an icon rather than becoming a presence in most people's minds—except her own, of course. She was hospitalized more than once for mental illness—a victim perhaps of her own elusiveness, a victim certainly (and no less so than Betty Hutton) of the image-making process as it was heedlessly conducted in Hollywood in the old days.

OPPOSITE: a quiet moment, c. 1943.
PAGE 56: in a grass skirt for *Son of Fury*, 1942.
PAGE 57: pouting to publicize *Sundown*, 1941.
PAGES 58–59: lounging in a negligee, 1942.

Betty Hutton was a funny girl —no question about that—but there was something touchingly naive about her, too. It was a quality Preston Sturges brilliantly brought out in his great 1944 comedy The Miracle of Morgan's Creek, *in which Hutton gave (virgin) birth to sextuplets. Paramount, alas, did not get the subtleties of her message. They saw her mainly as a madcap klutz, a young woman whose eager energy propelled her into situations in which she was reduced to shambles. Alternatively, they tried to sell her as yet another "blonde bombshell"—one who exploded not with sexuality but with hysteria.*

About none of this has she ever publicly commented. All we know is that her reputation for being "difficult" grew quickly and that her film career was essentially completed in a single decade. Later, she was declared bankrupt, and disappeared for years. She was then discovered working as a cook and housekeeper in a Catholic rectory in Rhode Island—the $10 million she was said to have made in the movies nowhere to be found.

It may be that her unhappy later life colors these pictures so poignantly. But even if she had survived Hollywood more happily, one would sense the desperation in these images—the inherent inhumanity of these self-consciously "nutty," hopelessly unfunny inventions.

OPPOSITE: pretty and serene, c. 1947.
PAGE 62: off in the wild, c. 1944.
PAGE 63: out on the field, c. 1944.

Ready to pop, c. 1944.

Ready to hop, 1952.

Ready to stomp, c. 1944.

But still a sweetheart, c. 1950.

Home. Hearth. Spaniels. Children. Maybe even apple pie. Beginning in the democratizing '30s movie stars ceased to flaunt their good fortune by building Graustarkian castles in the air above Beverly Hills. Now the studios wanted them to be seen as regular guys and gals, living like the suburbanizing middle class in comfier fantasies inspired by the cottages of Cape Cod or the ranch houses of the West. There were publicists from the old days who would later contend that Hollywood lost some of its hold on the public when it began to pretend that its stars were so distressingly ordinary.

But by not revealing the way the stars inflated the architectural models they followed, or whatever tensions underlay the scenes of family bliss staged within these walls, the stillsmen created another sort of fantasy—a dream of prosperous domesticity—that may have been even more potent. Yes, their subjects were shown to be able to indulge their whims— Martha Raye's oversized train set, Edward G. Robinson's art collection. But study his exemplary sobriety. And Glenn Ford's. And look! Here's the Ladd family gathering supportively around Dad— just like normal folks—as he packs for a business trip. And here's Rhonda Fleming's doctor husband, William Morril, sharing his medical library with their enviably well-behaved son. Who would dare to hold, against this evidence, that Hollywood was a den of licentiousness—or even of vulgar display?

Ronald Reagan welcomes the gang, c. 1942.

OPPOSITE: Martha Raye, 1940.

Bette Davis explores the dictionary with daughter Margot, c. 1964.

And shows how she does her own housework, c. 1964.

OPPOSITE: the picture of happiness—Jayne Mansfield, Mickey Hargitay, and baby son Miklos, 1958.
PAGE 70: Rhonda Fleming observes as husband, Thomas Lane, explains the *Materia Medica* to their son, Kent, c. 1945.
PAGE 71: Elizabeth Taylor ready for a quiet evening at home, 1954.
PAGES 72–73: the Ladds—Alan, wife Sue Carol, daughter Alana, and son David—1948.
PAGE 74: Patricia Ellis taking the sun, c. 1938.
PAGE 75: Johnny Mack Brown at the door, c. 1940.
PAGES 76 AND 77: the gentlemen and their collections—Edward G. Robinson, c. 1943, and Glenn Ford, 1946.

ABOVE RIGHT: Robert Walker with sons Bobby and
Michael, c. 1949.
RIGHT: Tom Drake, 1945.
OPPOSITE: Spencer Tracy, c. 1939.

Why a leopard (to vary Chico's famous query)? Or, to put the question more specifically, why were female stars and starlets more often linked symbolically with this big cat than with the others?

Like so many matters having to do with the movies, it was mostly a matter of image—but in this case, it was the image of the animal as much as that of the stars it was linked with. In mythology lions always seem to be roaring with impotent masculine rage, and burning-bright tigers are always threatening to ingest some passing pilgrim. But there is something playful in the sinuosity of the exotic and enigmatic leopard—if not sinfully, then at least suggestively so.

Perhaps, then, a woman—a "sex kitten"—pictorially associated with such a creature takes on this same quality. And maybe some others as well. One imagines the possibilities of gently clawing entwinement, for example. Or this thought occurs: that in the right hands she could become what any properly domesticated cat becomes—a bit of prettily purring plush, a pussy galor(ious), to twist a more recently famous movie name.

Venus in furs? Venus on fur? No, into the darker reaches of Middle Europe's imaginings we will not journey. These pictures were Made in America in a sweeter, sunnier time.

Jayne Mansfield promoting *Promises! Promises!*, c. 1963.

OPPOSITE: Gene Tierney, 1954.

Marion Carr, 1954.

OPPOSITE: Joan Collins, 1958.
OVERLEAF: Rhonda Fleming, c. 1944.

PORTRAIT OF A GIRL WITH ONE WHITE SHOE

Gloria Grahame, c. 1955.

Nowadays, hats require an explanation. When these pictures were made, they demanded a joke. Popular culture was rife with gags about the dithers women would get into over the choice of a new hat. Their anxiety on this subject showed women to be slaves to the decrees of "Dame Fashion" (to borrow a favorite newsreel locution), and this slavery was proof of their frivolity. It was proof, as well, that their views on weightier matters need not be taken seriously.

The typical American woman of these times did take an interest in the latest outrages of such famous milliners as Hattie Carnegie and Mr. John. But there was something bemused, almost anthropological, in this study. The few women who in real life donned the latest "chapeaus" did so with an air of conscious bravery—flinging back the male's contempt with a bold assertion of femininity.

Movie publicists catered impartially to both sexes. They placed pretty hats on pretty little heads for other women to study. They placed silly hats on silly little heads for men to chortle over. Now, though, we may regard woman's slipping out from under all her hats as an act of liberation no less consequential than her escape from girdles and cruelly wired bras.

CLOCKWISE FROM TOP LEFT: Thelma Ritter, c. 1959; Linda Darnell, c. 1941; Ellen Drew, 1940; Gene Tierney, c. 1944; Shirley Temple, 1944; Yvonne De Carlo, c. 1945. OPPOSITE: Dorothy Lamour, c. 1942.

TOP: Deanna Durbin, 1941.
ABOVE: Sophia Loren, 1966.
OPPOSITE: Jayne Mansfield, c. 1957.

TOP: Joan Crawford, c. 1948.
ABOVE: Ginger Rogers, 1946.

I n the world according to *AT&T, the telephone is an entirely unmixed and asexual blessing, allowing us to reach out and touch Grandpa and Grandma back on the farm or the kids away at college. It does not catch beautiful women in their negligees, halfway between bath and bed. Nor are such women supposed to pick up the phone and call men at such moments just because they happen to be feeling close to their skins.*

In the world according to our fantasies, though, such things happen all the time. And, truth to tell, reality feeds those imaginings. For everyday experience teaches us that the telephone is always intruding on our most intimate moments. And that it is precisely when we think we are getting comfortable only to ease the process of curling up with a good book that we are most likely to make a wicked call— one that is sure to get us into a lot of lovely trouble.

The pictures in this section suggest that even remote and beautiful women experience such moments, though of course the mute images do not tell us whether they are making the call or receiving it. Which is no matter, really. Both situations throatily whisper of the possibility of auditory as well as visual voyeurism. If only we knew their unlisted phone numbers! If only they knew our listed ones! What chin music we could be making together!

Gina Lollobrigida, c. 1962.

OPPOSITE: Muriel Barr, 1939.
PAGE 94: Linda Darnell, c. 1943.
PAGE 95: Shelley Winters, c. 1952.
PAGES 96–97: Alexis Smith, c. 1943.
PAGE 98: Rhonda Fleming, c. 1953.
PAGE 99: Marilyn Monroe, c. 1950.

What can one say? Flowers are pretty. Flowers are sweet. Flowers are nice. Flowers are conveniently ubiquitous in California. And, let's face it, flowers are a little boring.

For the likes of the ladies on these pages, the problem was to get away from such uninspired imagery, to imply that they were more than just another attractive bloom on Hollywood's vine. Jinx had to find Tex and go into radio in order to do so. Alice, despite her marriage to funny bandleader Phil Harris, never did. She was (and is) forever trapped in our minds, as she was in the studio's, as an old-fashioned girl, warbling an old-fashioned tune in nostalgic musicals. Olivia, also regarded by her bosses as every inch the sort of lady who did not survive the nineteenth century, went to court to escape their contractual hold, and eventually she proved she could act up to Oscar level, though never with the same spunky wit that she exhibited in her five costarring roles with Errol Flynn or opposite Cagney in Strawberry Blonde.

As for Duke Wayne, we've got to think he was kidding, or at least going along with an inspired gag, for no actor in Hollywood history ever had less reason to change his image, or less hope of doing so by tucking himself into a bower of flowers. Still, there is an odd appropriateness in this picture, in which he transcends its genre as effectively as he often did that of the Western.

Top: Jinx Falkenberg, c. 1946.
Above: Alice Faye, c. 1943.

Above: John Wayne, 1948.
Opposite: Olivia de Havilland, c. 1943.

Somehow this section saddens. Of these favored pairs who once mimed their mutual bliss for the portraitists, not one survives intact.

It is not the divorces that untimely sundered some of them that make us melancholy. We all knew Hollywood marriages wouldn't last. In our moral bookkeeping we implicitly understood that brevity of union was the price these handsome, spirited, lucky people usually paid for coupling. They didn't expect to have everything, did they?

No, it is death that stings, for it is difficult to associate with these lives. Of all the people in all of history who achieved fame, it is movie stars who have attained the most perfect immortality, the only ones whose work keeps not just the products of their talents before us, but their living, breathing, speaking presences as well. (It is, perhaps, the largest fringe benefit of the work—and the one that most surprised its recipients.) So it is when we contemplate such evidence as these pictures—reminders that these uniquely favored few led, or tried to lead, commonplace lives as well, therefore endured the frets and frustrations no one, no matter how gifted or graceful, can elude—that we see their humanity full and plain. And with a poignancy that extends even to Trigger stuffed in Roy Rogers's museum near bleak Barstow or to Charlie McCarthy silent on a shelf somewhere.

Danny Kaye and Sylvia Fine, c. 1941.

OPPOSITE: Ronald Reagan and Jane Wyman, c. 1945 (top); Dick Powell and Joan Blondell, c. 1940 (bottom left); Bogie and Betty, c. 1947 (bottom right).
PAGE 104: Pev Marle and Linda Darnell, c. 1943.
PAGE 105: Robert Taylor and Barbara Stanwyck, c. 1940.
PAGE 106: Tony Curtis and Janet Leigh, 1953.
PAGE 107: Eddie Fisher and Debbie Reynolds, 1955.
PAGES 108–109: Roy Rogers and Trigger, c. 1945.
PAGE 110: Tyrone Power and Annabella, c. 1940.
PAGE 111: Charlie McCarthy and Edgar Bergen, c. 1938.

Mona Freeman, c. 1948.

This is the essence of movie stardom: to live constantly surrounded by images of yourself—larger than life and stranger than fiction.

It is surprising how many stars had portraits of themselves in their homes; you would have thought that in private they might have enjoyed surcease from the replicated self. Still, you can see that most of these portraits were the work of painters who searched more assiduously than the studio photographers did for true essences rather than false or easy ones.

It is not surprising how often the stillsmen posed performers with images of themselves. This is a variation on the portrait-with-mirror convention, virtually as old as art itself. The advantage the Hollywood craftsmen had over their predecessors was the rich variety of reflections and refractions they could work with. Very few women, after all, have had dolls made up in their likeness, as Martha Raye did. Even fewer posed for a representation of themselves as universally recognized as Betty Grable's high-heels and latex pin-up pose, with which she here favorably compares her latter-day self.

Looking at these photos, one thinks of the little girl on the label, carrying a package of Morton's salt, which, of course, has a picture of her toting another salt box, which. . . . With these pictures Hollywood was suggesting that its products, too, poured forth, rain or shine, unto infinity.

Susan Hayward, 1967.

Alida Valli, 1947.

OPPOSITE: Lana Turner, 1942.

OPPOSITE: Paulette Goddard, c. 1943.
PAGE 118: Marlene Dietrich, c. 1953.
PAGE 119: Betty Grable in front of the 1941 pin-up, 1948.

Tony Perkins, c. 1960.

Opposite: Martha Raye, c. 1938.

U ntil the movies came along, it was easy to support the notion that there was something inherently unhealthy about acting. The theater, after all, is a nighttime activity, taking place under artificial light and requiring its players to resort to the artifices of make-up and curious costumes.

The movies could contradict all that—they needed to. They were made, or so it seemed, by daylight, and, especially after sound came in, they were acted by stars who seemed to be as real, as "natural," as the folks next door. (Never mind the prodigies of craft required to create these illusions.) Moreover, the movie capital was in far-off Los Angeles, to most Americans of the '30s and '40s an exotic realm where the sunshine was perpetual and the salubrities of sea and mountains and the soul-cleansing desert were enviably near at hand.

What could be more humanizing than to portray the stars as sportsmen and women (whose activities often required them to shed some of their clothes) taking advantage of these blessings? And these poses belied the gossip about wild parties and long nights at Mocambo and Ciro's.

Oh, the leaps of faith we must have taken beholding these pictures, so many of them so obviously studio shots. Sophisticated Barbara Stanwyck as a canoeist? Sweet, tormented Judy Garland as a shootist? Sexy Rita Hayworth as a badminton buff? Dreamy— we could do all that stuff, and imagine doing it with them— but improbable.

OPPOSITE: Barbara Stanwyck, 1949.
PAGE 124: Judy Garland, c. 1940.
PAGE 125: Guy Madison, c. 1944.

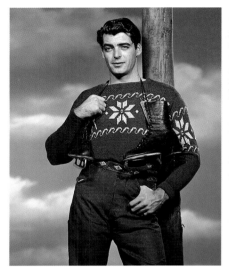

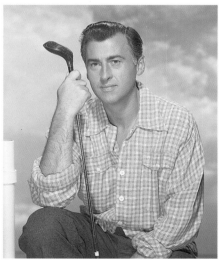

CLOCKWISE FROM TOP LEFT: Rory Calhoun, 1947;
Rosalind Russell, c. 1938; Elizabeth Taylor, c. 1951;
Stewart Granger, 1950; Barbara Bates, 1945; Olivia de
Havilland, 1940.
OPPOSITE: Rita Hayworth, 1939.

We know something about the beginnings of Jean Peters's public life; she was chosen Miss Ohio State when she was in college and received a trip to Hollywood as her prize. We know something about the effective end of that life; she began keeping company with reclusive Howard Hughes, retired from the movies probably at his insistence, married him in 1957, and divorced him in 1971, having given him what might have been the best years of her screen life.

Between discovery and marriage she was a "movie star." That is to say, she was under contract to Fox and made a number of movies in which she received billing above the title. But she was never a movie star in our hearts—mostly because, like the studio, we could never quite figure out who she was or what she was supposed to represent.

This collection of stills is a record of how hard her employers worked to establish a profitable persona for her. Was she, perhaps, another in the extensive family of girls next door? No, wait a minute, she's an outdoorsy type. Wrong again, she's a siren. Nope, she's really a rather pious sort. That's where she ended up—as a minister's wife in A Man Called Peter, her last film.

One imagines Peters as glad to leave it at that. And one apologizes for typing her one last time—as a symbol of all the pretty girls the movies called but the public refused to choose, no matter how hard the studios worked on their images.

OPPOSITE: Jean Peters—the country girl look—c. 1953.
PAGE 130, CLOCKWISE FROM TOP LEFT: the sexy look, 1949; the sporty look, 1951; the sultry look—for *Pickup on South Street*—1953; and the saintly look—for *A Man Called Peter*—1955.
PAGE 131: New Year's Day pin-up, 1947.

Shall we speak, then, of Jeffersonian democracy, and its belief that in our rural yeomanry there reposed the best American values, especially in contrast to the city's slickers? Perhaps not in the present context.

Well, then, should we instead mention the yearning of recently urbanized America for the sunswept serenity, the sweet simplicities it left behind on the farms and in the small towns? Maybe later.

All right, then, how about innocence, female innocence? That has always been one of bucolic America's major cash crops—especially in song, story, and film representations of it. It's good to associate a star with that, especially one like Doris Day, who was the Mary Pickford of the '50s and early '60s until the whole nation, overdosed, started going into insulin shock when she appeared.

But wait. What about the Farmer's Daughter—Innocence's comic sister, whose existence was recognized only by a wink and a joke? We can't ignore her. And Hollywood did not. It only looks as if Betty Grable is kicking over those milk cans. What she's really kicking over is the traces. And reminding us that in the dark, at the movies, all males have something of the traveling salesman about them.

Betty Grable, 1953.

OPPOSITE: Doris Day, c. 1956.

No one has ever been more intensely ruled by the calendar than the men behind Hollywood's portrait cameras. There is a holiday, official or unofficial, almost every month of the year. And there used to be an insatiable need among the nation's Sunday editors for imagery to mark those occasions on the covers of their Sunday magazine sections or their screen and radio and, latterly, television guides.

The competition for this choicest of space was obviously intense. Yet here, more than anywhere else in the stillsman's realm, originality was seemingly discouraged. Here convention ruled. A thousand starlets stepped through a January calendar page to mark the turning of the year, another thousand reclined against a Valentine's heart. Hundreds more toyed with a phallic rocket to celebrate the glorious Fourth or perched perkily atop a pumpkin to welcome Halloween. Or felt the scratch of a Christmas tree against her bare thighs as she nestled into it for the lensman.

In other words, we insisted on these solemn occasions that Hollywood stick to the iconographic rules that the rest of us observed when we decorated for the great days. You guys can have all the fun you want the rest of a year; but tradition is tradition and, dammit, there are times when it must be served. Bless everybody's hearts. Holidays just aren't holidays since these pictures went away.

OPPOSITE: Janis Paige, New Year's Eve, 1948.
PAGE 136: Yvonne De Carlo, Valentine's Day, c. 1945.
PAGE 137: Deanna Durbin, Valentine's Day, 1947.
PAGE 138: June Haver, St. Patrick's Day, c. 1944.
PAGE 139: Margaret O'Brien, Easter, 1943.
PAGE 140: Adele August, Fourth of July, 1955.
PAGE 141: Virginia Dole, Fourth of July, 1942.
PAGE 142: Ann Rutherford, Halloween, c. 1941.
PAGE 143: Donna Reed, Thanksgiving, 1941.
PAGE 144: Rosemary and Priscilla Lane, Christmas, 1938.
PAGE 145: Lassie, Christmas, 1945.
PAGE 146: Mary Martin, Christmas, c. 1942.
PAGE 147: Deanna Durbin, Christmas, c. 1938.

Marilyn Monroe, c. 1948.

The authors acknowledge with thanks the cooperation of the following film companies: Columbia Pictures, Goldwyn Pictures, MGM, Paramount Pictures, Republic Pictures, RKO, Selznick Productions, 20th Century-Fox, United Artists, Universal, Hal Wallis Productions, Walter Wanger Productions, and Warner Bros.

The book is dedicated to all the photographers who made *Striking Poses* possible: Jack Albin, Virgil Apger, Ernest Bachrach, Bruce Bailey, Carlyle Blackwell, Jr., Clarence Sinclair Bull, Eric Carpenter, Bob Coburn, Cronenweth, Eliot Elisofon, John Engstead, Bud Fraker, Roman Freulich, Ray Jones, Gene Korman, Madison Lacy, Floyd McCarthy, John Miehle, Frank Powolny, E. R. Richee, A. L. "Whitey" Schafer, Ned Scott, Bert Six, and Scotty Welbourne.

PAGE 1: Paramount/photo by Bob Coburn
2: Columbia
7: Columbia/photo by Bob Coburn
9: 20th Century-Fox
10: Columbia
11: MGM
13: RKO/photo by Carlyle Blackwell, Jr.
14: Phil Stern
16: Paramount
17, CLOCKWISE FROM TOP LEFT: Paramount; Warner Bros./photo by Floyd McCarthy; Warner Bros.; Columbia
18–19: Columbia
20: Columbia/photo by Cronenweth
21: RKO/photo by Crosby
22, 23: 20th Century-Fox
25: Columbia
27: Goldwyn/photo by Ernest Bachrach
28, CLOCKWISE FROM TOP: Paramount; Warner Bros.; Columbia/photo by Bob Coburn
29: 20th Century-Fox
30: Paramount
31: Paramount/photo by Frank Powolny
32: Paramount
33: Paramount/photo by Bud Fraker
34: MGM
35: Universal
36: 20th Century-Fox
37, CLOCKWISE FROM TOP: 20th Century-Fox/photo by Frank Powolny; MGM/photo by Clarence Sinclair Bull; for *The Girl from Avenue A*, 20th Century-Fox
38, LEFT TO RIGHT: 20th Century-Fox/photo by Frank Powolny; MGM
39: MGM/photo by Clarence Sinclair Bull

40: Paramount/photo by Bud Fraker
41: Warner Bros./photo by Bert Six
42: 20th Century-Fox/photo by Frank Powolny
43: Paramount/photo by Bud Fraker
44, LEFT TO RIGHT: MGM/photo by Eric Carpenter; 20th Century-Fox
45: MGM/photo by Virgil Apger
46: Universal/photo by Ray Jones
47: Columbia
48: 20th Century-Fox
49: Columbia/photo by Bob Coburn
50: MGM/photo by Eric Carpenter
51: Paramount
53: 20th Century-Fox
55, 56: 20th Century-Fox
57: Walter Wanger Productions for United Artists/photo by Bob Coburn
58–59: 20th Century-Fox/photo by Jack Albin
61, 62, 63, 64 (BOTH), 65 (LEFT): Paramount/photos by Bud Fraker
65, RIGHT: Paramount
66: Warner Bros.
67: Paramount
68 (BOTH): Warner Bros.
69: 20th Century-Fox/photo by Frank Powolny
70: Selznick Productions/photo by John Miehle
71: MGM/photo by Virgil Apger
72–73: Paramount
74: Warner Bros.
75: for *Bury Me Not on the Lonesome Prairie*, Universal/photo by Bruce Bailey
76: Warner Bros.
77: Columbia/photo by Ned Scott

78 (BOTH): MGM/photo by Virgil Apger
79: MGM/photo by Eric Carpenter
80: Noonan-Taylor Productions for NTD
81: 20th Century-Fox/photo by Frank Powolny
82: Warner Bros./photo by Bert Six
83: 20th Century-Fox/photo by Frank Powolny
84–85: Selznick Productions/photo by Madison Lacy
87: United Artists
88, CLOCKWISE FROM TOP LEFT: Paramount; 20th Century-Fox/photo by Frank Powolny; for *Buck Benny Rides Again*, Paramount/photo by A. L. ''Whitey'' Schafer; 20th Century-Fox/photo by Frank Powolny; Selznick Productions/photo by John Miehle; Universal/photo by Roman Freulich
89: Paramount/photo by A. L. ''Whitey'' Schafer
90: 20th Century-Fox
91, CLOCKWISE FROM TOP LEFT: Universal/photo by Ray Jones; Warner Bros./photo by Bert Six; Universal/photo by Ray Jones; Universal
92: MGM/photo by Virgil Apger
93: Paramount/photo by E. R. Richee
94: 20th Century-Fox/photo by John Engstead
95: for *Phone Call from a Stranger*, 20th Century-Fox/photo by Gene Korman
96–97: Warner Bros./photo by Scotty Welbourne
98: Paramount/photo by Bud Fraker
99: 20th Century-Fox/photo by Frank Powolny
100, CLOCKWISE FROM TOP: Columbia/photo by Bob Coburn; Republic Pictures/photo by Roman Freulich; 20th Century-Fox/photo by Gene Korman
101: Warner Bros./photo by Scotty Welbourne
102: Goldwyn/photo by Bob Coburn
103, CLOCKWISE FROM TOP: Warner Bros.; Warner Bros./photo by Jack Albin; Warner Bros./photo by E. R. Richee
104: 20th Century-Fox
105: MGM/photo by Eric Carpenter
106: Universal/photo by Ray Jones
107: MGM/photo by Virgil Apger
108–109: Republic Pictures/photo by Roman Freulich

110: 20th Century-Fox/photo by Jack Albin
111: Goldwyn/photo by Bob Coburn
113: Paramount/photo by A. L. ''Whitey'' Schafer
114, LEFT TO RIGHT: 20th Century-Fox; Selznick Productions/photo by John Miehle
115: MGM/photo by Eliot Elisofon
116–117: Paramount/painting in background by Diego Rivera
118: unknown
119: Paramount/both photos (the old and the new) by Frank Powolny
120, 121: Paramount
123: Hal Wallis Productions for Paramount
124: MGM/photo by Eric Carpenter
125: Selznick Productions/photo by John Miehle
126, CLOCKWISE FROM TOP LEFT: Selznick Productions/photo by John Miehle; MGM/photo by Clarence Sinclair Bull; MGM/photo by Virgil Apger; MGM/photo by Virgil Apger; Universal/photo by Ray Jones; Warner Bros.
127: Columbia
129: 20th Century-Fox/photo by Frank Powolny
130 (ALL), 131: 20th Century-Fox
132: for *The Farmer Takes a Wife*, 20th Century-Fox/photo by Frank Powolny
133: MGM/photo by Virgil Apger
135: Warner Bros./photo by E. R. Richee
136, 137: Universal/photos by Ray Jones
138: for *Irish Eyes Are Smiling*, 20th Century-Fox
139: MGM/photo by Clarence Sinclair Bull
140: Columbia/photo by Cronenweth
141: Paramount/photo by A. L. ''Whitey'' Schafer
142: MGM
143: MGM/photo by Clarence Sinclair Bull
144: Warner Bros.
145: MGM/photo by Clarence Sinclair Bull
146: Paramount/photo by E. R. Richee
147: Universal/photo by Ray Jones
149: 20th Century-Fox

The color plates in this book were laser-scanned from original negatives and transparencies. Great care has been taken in the reproduction of the plates, but the delicate and, in some cases, unstable nature of the originals has given rise to occasional unavoidable blemishes and unevenness in some of the reproductions.

Composed in Devinne and Gill Sans medium condensed by Arkotype Inc., New York, New York

Printed and bound by Dai Nippon Printing Co., Ltd., Tokyo, Japan